NIGHTS OF NAKED MANNEQUINS

NIGHTS OF NAKED MANNEQUINS

POEMS BY

MICHAEL LEE PHILLIPS

AUSTIN HALL PRESS
Trona, California

NIGHTS OF NAKED MANNEQUINS

Copyright © 2010 by Michael Lee Phillips. All rights reserved.
Printed in the United States of America.
No part of this book may be used or reproduced in any manner whatsoever
without written permission except in the case of brief quotations in critical articles and reviews.
Direct all enquiries to Austin Hall Press, Box 935, Trona, California, 93562 or editors@austinhallpress.com.

Library of Congress Control Number: 2001012345

ISBN 061535694X

EAN-13 978-0-615-35694-5

APPRECIATION: First of all, I would like to acknowledge Peg Shaen, who was there at the beginning and whose help will never be forgotten. I would like to thank a few of the guys who heard some of these stories before they became poems: Bob, Bill, Frank, Novascone, Darrel, Andy. Thanks again to Bob Shaen for his timely and perceptive suggestions and also to Bill Manatt for his warnings. Thanks also to Margaret for help with weekly chores that kept things moving. Most of all, I owe everything to Susie, whose expertise and aesthetic wisdom always held true.

Acknowledgments

Grateful acknowledgment is made to the editors of the following publications where these poems or earlier versions of them appeared or will appear.

Beloit Poetry Journal: "The Women on Rhodes"

Caveat Lector: "Flash"

Chiron Review: "Red '59 Ford Pickup"
"The Pod"

Cider Press Review: "Godpowers & Choice"

Cimarron Review: "The Nymphomaniac"

Connecticut Review: "Sailing Along"

Descant: "Keith Richards Is Still a Friend of Mine"

High Plains Literary Review: "Slo-Pitch in Chinook, Washington"

The New York Quarterly:
"Milking Maid"
"The Hierarchal Binaries of Ron Jeremy: an Ode"
"Faces Sing, and Louder Sing, at the Reunion"

Pearl: "The New World"

Poetry Northwest: "Scorpion Love"

Southern Poetry Review: "The Tongue and the Blonde"

*The Stinging Fly (*Ireland): "A Prayer for Nikos Kazantzakis"

Yellow Silk: "Cape Sounion"
"Children Left in the Palm of Your Hand"

*In the very essence of poetry there is something indecent:
a thing is brought forth which we didn't know we had in us...*

Czeslaw Milosz, "Ars Poetica?"

I asked her for water, she brought me gasoline.

Howlin' Wolf

CONTENTS

I

The Beast Rises, with Little Discourse 3
Keith Richards Is Still a Friend of Mine 4
The New World 6
Forecast 8
Cold Pizza 9
Tides 10
Scorpion Love 11
Breakfast at Denny's 12
Sap 15
The Hierarchal Binaries of Ron Jeremy: An Ode 16
Haiku Sunset #22 and the Lost Lover 18
Milking Maid 20
Naked 22

Sweet Things   26
On the Beach   28
Nights of Naked Mannequins   30

II

Stanza One   35
Children Left in the Palm of Your Hand   38
Cape Sounion   39
Syrup   40
Trains and Philosophy   42
The Nymphomaniac   44
The Pod   46
The Black Poem   48
Coffee   50
Sunset in Shades of Desire   52
Two Lattes   54
Slo-Pitch in Chinook, Washington   55
Separate Rooms   56
The Gym for Settling Old Scores   57
What's Forgotten, What's Not   58
The Women on Rhodes   60
Old Sage & the Bitch   62
The Point   64

III

Laundry   69
Phones   71
Marmaris Cafe   73
Flash   74
Bound for Athens   75
Arrows   77
Red '59 Ford Pickup   81
Godpowers & Choice   83
Quality Time   84

IV

The Tongue and the Blonde 89
A Prayer for Nikos Kazantzakis 90
Pantoum of Sex 91
Toasting the Monsters 92
Every Good Story 94
Segues 96
Love's Passport 99
The Cow Never Seen in a Photograph 103
Faces Sing, and Louder Sing, at the Reunion 105
In the Sangre de Cristo Mountains 107
The Mohs Scale 109
Sailing Along 113
The Beast in Decline Shares His Vision 114

For Susie,

love

of my life

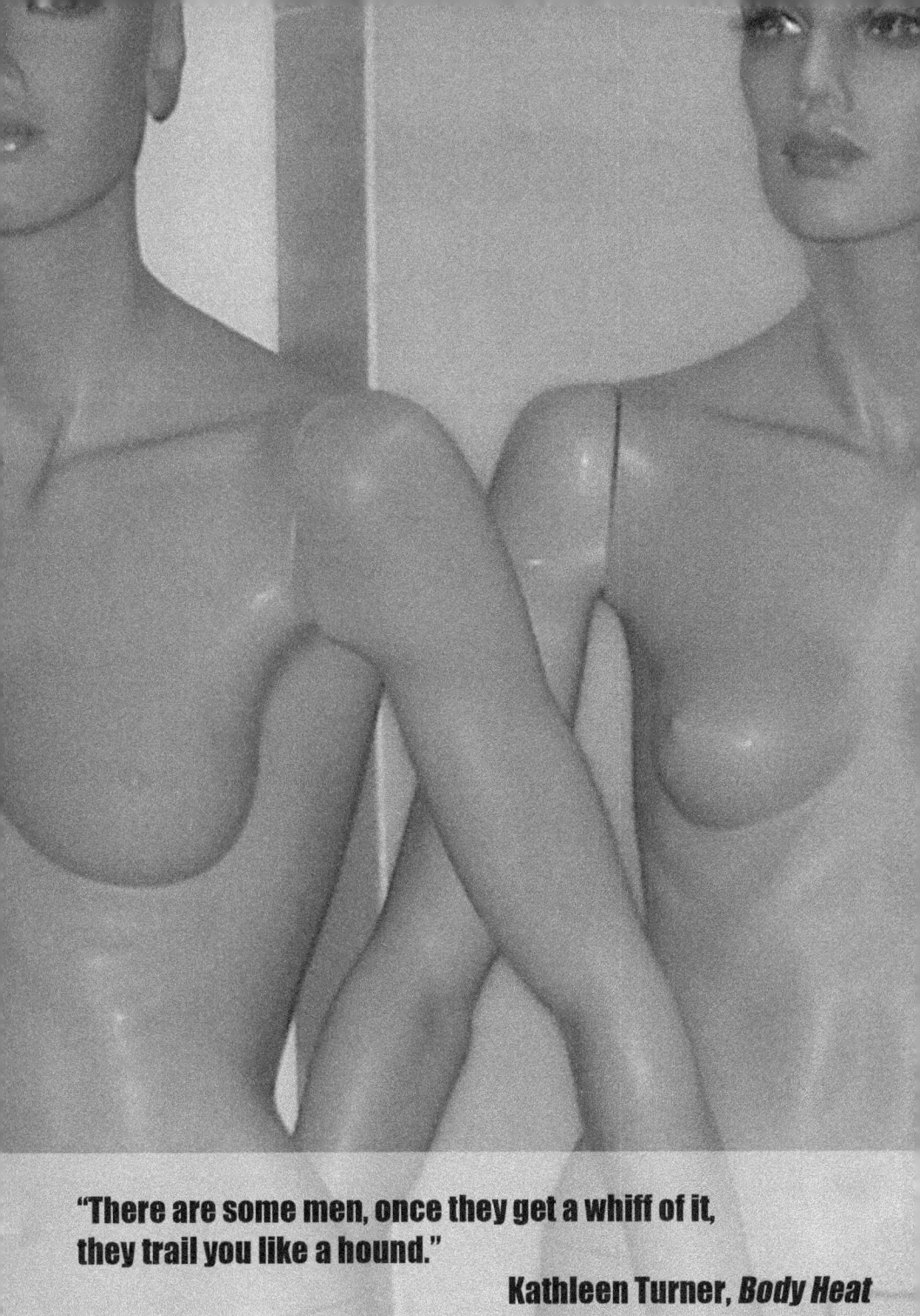

The Beast Rises, with Little Discourse

It was amazing
the way
biology suddenly
took over
one night
so long ago –

as if to say
enough of
this shit,
I'm going to
get laid.

And somewhere
in that first dream
of nakedness I
came all over
myself,
spilling into
underwear, sheets,
the mattress.

For the
rest of the
night I groaned
and wallowed
in that goo
like some new beast
in a mud hole
out on an African veldt –
finally, finally
come alive.

Keith Richards Is Still a Friend of Mine

It's a fifty-six Chevy Bel Air, four door,
windshield still cracked by a hood ornament
blown off in a bad wind outside Mojave.
Front seat covered in slippery vinyl, and it's
the sweaty August of a deadly summer:
Watts has burned itself into black and white
on the living room TV for the past two nights,
and from somewhere across the Pacific comes
ominous news of body counts and body bags.
But tonight the 'mighty five-ninety' station
out of San Bernardino keeps *Satisfaction*
alive in every car near the Inland Empire,
even mine, the radio being an AM only
piece of shit, reception fading in and
out between the surf of static. And she says,
"Are those the Trona Pinnacles, those spiky
shadows over there?" Turning her head
away leaving even the neck hard to kiss,
clearly not buying into the decadent
possibilities of our isolation. The whole
night one long priapic finagling with
the prudish defenses conscripted by
good parenting – a smooch here, smooch
there, the giggles and, one assumed,
the blushing whenever my tongue scored
a hit. Until: with a marrow-numbed
right arm between the seat and her shoulders,
the steering wheel ground into a bruised
left hip, the whole body about to cramp
from its defeated contortion in a moment
of surrender, the deejay's voice hopped onto
a wave of guitars curling out of the dial,

and, static-free, Keith's signature
chords thumped from the dash like
the boom box of a great heart. I heard
her take in her breath and felt her
hold it. When she let it out, her face
lifted to mine and I could see all
the fight was gone. "I just love that song,"
she said, the giggles now deeper and
making no apologies for everything
about to happen. When her shy fingers
began to fumble with my zipper,
I knew he had changed my life forever.

THE NEW WORLD

The first time I went down on someone
she was still a girl,
wouldn't be a woman for years.
I was still a boy,
wouldn't be a man for god knows how long.

It was summer – we lay on a blanket
out behind the garage
shorts down at the ankles ready to come up fast
at any suspicious sound.

I had never heard of the clitoris that first time,
and neither had she.
The word wasn't out yet –
even women's magazines were mum on that.

I set sail into her wetness like some adolescent Columbus,
looking for treasures I couldn't imagine,
lost the whole time.
But I got lucky, too, just like Columbus.

Found something unexpected –
yes, there, don't stop, she told me as soon as I drifted
onto that small island of pleasure.
And, of course, I didn't,
even though the seas became, let us say, a bit turbulent.

And when I returned to her kisses to report
what I had discovered, she smiled
like a queen who understands, for the first time,
her inherited power.

She put one hand on my shoulder and pulled me closer.
Further expeditions, I could see,
were already approved.

Forecast

At the stoplight she tells him she's been wet
all morning & she slips her fingers
up her skirt between her legs
& he knows things will come to a head
here so to speak the light still being red

& his Jeep idling between a Beemer & a Mercedes
& it all being very Southern California
he thinks & even her skin so fashionably brown
& no tan lines & the Pacific off to the right
if he looked & he thinks again

no panties & by the time her glistening fingers
glide with just a twinkle of California sun
up to her mouth he knows
he's going to get hard of course what else
& when the light turns green everything
is a go & the Beemer & Mercedes
blasting ahead & his Jeep drifting to a slow lane

looking for an off-ramp & it's not long before
he's got her sticky fingers in his
mouth too & not long after that
her slick tongue is whispering something
in his ear & he's nodding of course & losing
sight of the road & she's out of her seat belt

& the wet tongue in his ear has moved
to his navel & it's dropping fast a barometer
of urgency & urges & a forecaster of inclement
desires & a slight precipitation already
leaking out & predictions of heavy showers to come

COLD PIZZA

The morning's early & you've got a cock
rightfully limp the tender tip
stuck by a gob of dried comeglue
to one of her buttocks
& arms & legs
are everywhere in the dark
having disappeared
into body-twined numbness & all movement
now by rote or braille
the braille being somewhat retarded
due to numbness & all
& of course her body has cooled
yours too & dried overnight the melting
passion congealed & glazed &
your cock still stuck & still
shriveled & a certain smell everywhere
fingers lips & tongues
if one could smell them & stains too
all part of the effluvium
& sure enough there's a little purring
going on up above
you're not awake alone & moaning one might
even say & already
she's got fingers in the crust
so to speak & it seems everything now
even the unshrivelling cock
is eager for the first slice of morning
your tongue that sticky rascal
perhaps slow to warm
still raw after last night's feast
all the dessert etc.

Tides

So naked we were turned inside out.
Her cunt still moist
Still saying, once more, once more.

Sperm and joyful stickiness
Everywhere
The sea of it filling up the room.

Two of us floating on a mattress
Of everything we had given.

The sea rising up to the window.
Moon outside
Saying I want it all back.

The sea flowing out the window.
She, taking my hand,
Saying, come on, come on.

Two of us
Chasing the sea
Chasing the moon onto the beach.

Before we hit the first wave
We were already
Inside each other's skin.

Scorpion Love

And he would always love that moment, the way
She told him about the scorpion in their bed.
He felt her hair first, from behind, slide
Into his neck. Then a whisper and the voice,
Calmer than himself when he saw she was right.
Across the coiled rug and hardwood floor
A fire he would have to leave snapped behind
Its grate, the orange heat occupying space
It would never possess.

                      Outside, the aspens
Burned a new color for the night, and he thought
Of the rolled newspaper he would need, thought
of the scorpion he would soon remove, its
Crab-like posture sloped against a wrinkle,
The condemning stinger poised overhead.

What could that scorpion know of a fire
That had burned all evening just the way
It should? Had it ever noticed the chameleon
Leaves and how they played with the light
Dying over Carson Peak? Certainly it knew
Nothing of the way a woman would interrupt
A moment only to create another moment by telling
Him that it was there, alone in the bedroom,
Waiting in all its innocence to be killed.

Breakfast at Denny's

Been a long night
slipping & sliding &
now it's a Denny's booth
& Flo on the name tag left
thick aroma of America
a.m. eggs & potatoes & toast
& sausage & gravy & coffee &
besides that you've
got a bare foot stuck
in your crotch under the table
& you've been caressing
it like a warm tit Flo or no
& once again you think
you've discovered paradise &
who would have guessed Denny's
for such a venue

She's in her thrift shop
dancing outfit delicious
in her own right nouveau as hell
shift silky blouse no panties
& golden muff you assume still sticky
& you wonder could you
get it up again after last night
& morning also your balls
like vacuums ready to implode
& cock the tip crispy still
from a wake-up slide
& eager teeth all so new millennium

& you've agreed no more metaphors
love & sex both naked & free

emotions awake to the possibilities
mutual indices of desire
stripped down to hard-on &
wet cunt the adamant statement
flesh qua flesh heady stuff
here with the fragrances
of morning America hardhats
at the counter knowing
she's better than caffeine &
somewhere here you let slip
a thought a side order
of pique a condiment of provocation
that men are guides
women tourists menu of life
so to speak phallus
pointing the way undefeated
signifier of life weak coffee
slow to jumpstart the cognitive
a possible later defense
for the utterance but
breakfast qua breakfast instantly
problematic and deconstructing

portions of it doing so
right in your lap & the hot
stain sliding crotchward
even as she exits & Flo
still on the name tag at the booth
saying honey I seen it
all before & the hardhats achuckle
crude signifiers
over their safe caffeine &
her pacing outside already
the locked Jeep
igniting her molten face &

how can you tell Flo
still with her name tag it's
only a post something dilemma
the eternal romantic différence
over thick aroma of America a.m. eggs
& potatoes etc. & her out there clearly
defying conceptualization maybe
discourse too & you still inside eager
to leave but unable to move
& undecided over the menu
of fading narrative

Sap

It was a big, empty
rental house,
but the front door
opened like home.

Quiet block,
nice neighborhood.

Then she showed up
after
too many years.

All those trees
grown tall now
just so
we could fuck
like mad
on the floors
without being seen.

THE HIERARCHAL BINARIES OF RON JEREMY: AN ODE

Mention the video return &
she says my notions about her body
have been culturally encoded
& that starts it off again,
the morning I thought I had
disappearing into discourse

All so fashionably postmodern—
she's shouting objectification
something about her body
as narrative & I'm saying
didn't she mean decoded not encoded

It's all virgin/whore dichotomy
& patriarchal subjugation &
I can't keep it all straight
wondering if I'm
the signifier or referent today
& what does she mean
appropriating womanhood

Just a while ago it was naked breakfast
romantic you could go so far
soft touches
playful pinches
pats on the tummies
whispers, tongues, crazy stuff

Now it's all commodification,
phallic systems & just the same
it's her rental after all due

back today – there it is the counter
still blinking stopped halfway

Right after that long and famous cock
slipped from a frothing cunt
to glide into a waiting mouth
& chubby Ron off camera going oh yeah oh yeah
& the two of us on the couch
her in encoded or decoded flesh
reaching for my patriarchal cock
eager for the taste & nothing except
naked lust in her pretty little head

Haiku Sunset #22 and the Lost Lover

    From hills like your thighs
        The menarcheal sky bleeds
    Up to clouds like come:

The twenty-second because
the first twenty-one kept squirming
loose, the bloat verbiage defying
the anorexic form, one after
the other breaking down the frail
syllabic frames just like
the love you thought you had.
Too much weight for simple words,
like I love you she once scrawled
into the beach near her home.
It all being so long ago
you have to think hard to remember
her name, the weight of time,
you could say, too heavy
for the words to survive.
But the inspiration still fresh –
how she spread her legs one afternoon
on her hard futon and said,
taste it, and you smelled
the crimson streaks
sliding down her fingers
before you did, and her back
arched when your tongue went deep,
and her own tongue sought yours
when you came up, and the tongues
went crazy together. When it was
all over, she smiled at the mirror,
both of you bloodied like ten-round

survivors. And that's the way you slept,
and the first line came to you
on the drive home when you glanced
at the milky cumulus streaking
above the coast range. And the last
line came finally weeks later just
before her own visit, and how timely
you can think now, the last line
and the last time so synchronous,
the weight of that moment
too heavy for them both. And if
you knew where she drifted off to,
you'd tell her it's the same haiku,
the one she left behind in the bathroom,
bobby-pinned to the mirror,
x's lipsticked across the top
the words take care smudged at the bottom.
Here it is again, you'd like to tell her.
Give the little poem another chance,
sweetheart. Steal it if you need to.

Milking Maid

The two of you lying naked
& it's the first time for that &
the sea through the motel window
cheering it all on giving it
the foamy metaphor of approval.
Until a cruel reality pierces you
& you know deep down it won't last
& you ask her & you're sincere
& devoid of metaphor & honest yes
honest as you'll ever be & you ask
her in the future whenever it happens
when she meets that right guy
the knight in armor and all that
years from now but who knows
but when it happens & she's got
that first child in all honesty
you ask if she will send you milk
from her breasts FedEx overnight
or whatever & you'll reimburse her
too if that's a concern but enough
for a good gulp would she promise
& remember that it's the first time
& you're lying naked & the sea
is in on it too a tender moment &
she's young & wants to please
& she doesn't know you well yet
in fact never would & in her eyes
you can tell that she thinks it's
your humor more romantic banter

so she smiles & nods & says yes
& looking back now you can see
that was her first lie – or maybe not –
let's just say that you're still waiting.

Naked

she wanted to write
they all do at her age, it's worse than
the curse
so what are you waiting for, I said
these young ones always want
to write
they think wanting to
is the same
as writing

I write my thoughts in a journal
she said
of course you do honey, I said
that's what they all do
they write in journals
people make
fortunes
I tell you, fortunes
selling these
artsy journals
to young women, young women
who want to write –
invest in
journal
makers
I say

this one had latent feminist tendencies
don't they all
she knew
the jargon, up on all her
goddesses

she was freeing herself,
empowering herself, that too
liked to take her
clothes off
took them off a lot, in fact
for lots of people,
but here's
the truth, she didn't really like
being naked, naked
is something
else, being naked is harder
than taking off
your clothes

you can't write just by
taking
your clothes off, honey
to write
you have to be
naked, that means everything
heart, soul, all the fears, lusts, disasters
and crimes
out there on the page with spotlights
not just sans clothes

but this one, this one wanted
to write,
so she took her clothes off
that was a
start, took yours off
too
tried to get her naked
to show something besides the tits
you had a fire
in the fireplace, you were hamming it up
you brought out

the poetry, and you read
to each other
no clothes, trying to get to naked
I want to write
she insisted
that gave you no choice, you pulled
Bukowski
off the shelf
try this, you said
she had nice tits, wonderful ass, you
gave
her credit
there, you can't say anything about
her writing
that was all in
the journal, you see,
invest
in journals

but Bukowski
she balked at Bukowski, I don't think I should,
she said,
wasn't he a macho bastard, misogynist prick,
a real asshole,
a drunk?
true, I said
try it, and she opened her
mouth and Bukowski
went down her
like a
big cock, and
when he came she swallowed it all

I never knew it could
be like
this, she said afterwards,
too bad
he died

she was almost
naked

she thanked me

my pleasure
I said

Sweet Things

I wanted my cock inside your cunt
So bad
I would say anything.
Honey, you said, don't be crude.
Say something sweet, sweet things.

So I said sweet things.
Said them for years, it seems.
And you said them too. Honey,
You would say back then,
Honey, you're such a sweetie.

We were both being sweet, I guess.
And it was nice, as they say –
But let me confess, right now,
Before I forget. Even then,
When it was all so sweet,
Whenever you said that word, *honey,*
 I thought of your cunt,
Your cunt running wet, your cunt
Tasting pure ambrosia.

Of course, I never mentioned your cunt,
Or my cock.
But they found each other, now and then,
And from all accounts, it was sweet.
Stayed like that for a long time,
If you recall. Everything sweet.
You calling me honey. Telling me
How nice it all was. Me thinking
About your cunt, never telling you.

After you left (honey, it's just over)
All I could remember of you were those
Sweet words you left behind, stacked
Up outside us like cords of green wood.
Sticky with sap. Too damp to catch fire.

On the Beach

In the sand at
Carmel, the
clean white sand
of the beach,
she drew
a figure
with her finger.

What is that,
I asked.

It's my cunt,
she said.
Couldn't
you tell?

I bent down,
drove my
tongue deep
into it.

She laughed
as I licked
all the
way up. Afterwards,
I gagged and
spat out
the sand.

You're right,
I said.
It is
your
cunt.

Nights of Naked Mannequins

Three a.m.
and my hands
as I knew they would
leave their cleaning to begin another rape.

Skinny without diets
she never farts
and never bleeds
and can't resist.
I give her a name.

The hands take command.
No sudden blow
here. No great wings
beating still,

No feathered glory.
It's just habit, ritual,
an awkward
dumb show
performed each night
before an audience of dozing merchandise.

I press myself to her,
feel the statued passiveness
the plastic toughness
of her ass.

I ignore that she sprouts no hair,
that her breasts carry no nipples,
that her lips won't part,
and that my tongue, calloused by now,
licks at details her maker forgot.

I'm not proud.
I whisper her name
plead for unnatural acts.
And after –
I thank her for not crying out,
stoop to the vacuum
and sweep the uncleaned aisles
winking at frozen stares of her mounted sisters.

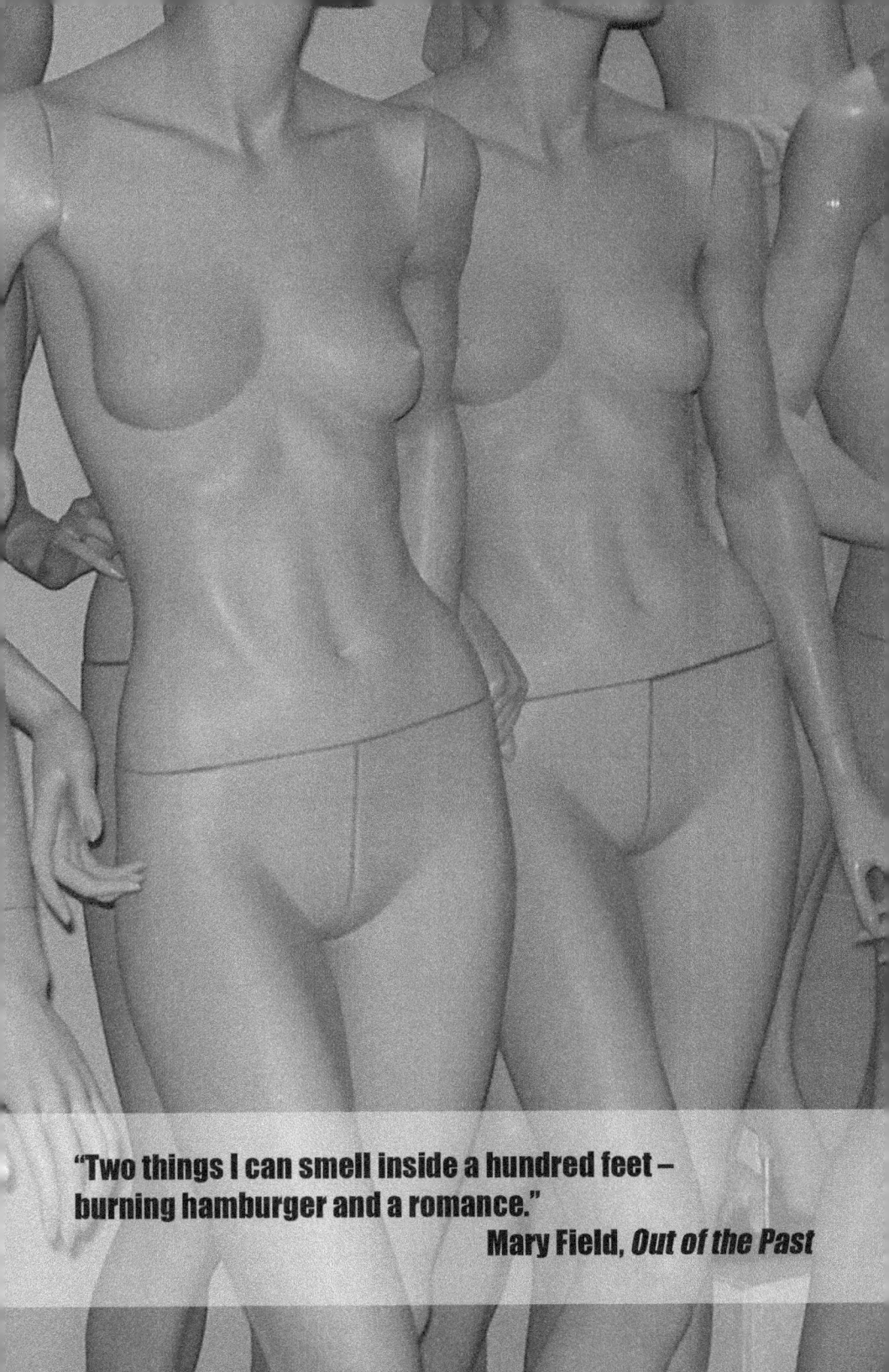

Stanza One

Anything can happen. So they say.
Expect the unexpected.
That's what they say.
You never know. They say
that too.

You've seen her before.
At least part of you believes that.

Just by chance
(see stanza one)
you're both in line at
a high-maintenance latte place.

Really, it's not your kind of venue.
Standing in line for gooey coffee
isn't your kind of thing.
But sometimes (see stanza one).

And here she is. Two of you chat
a bit: instantly, obviously,
she's not impressed.

You watch a boutique smile
mash into a trailer park grimace.
Suddenly she seems eager,
you might say, to beat a hasty retreat
out the door.

Truly a moment devoid of philosophical
conjunction—
not a whit of the cheeky badinage

that high end
latte places thrive upon.

Back at the apartment the mirror doesn't lie.
Ah reflections!
There it is.
Right there in the middle
of your shirt: big honkin' loogie!

A consequence you guess
of that morning's
Gorilla-like sneeze into Kleenex.

Green and pulpy and gross as hell,
a shiny viscousy
tail streaked above it, sort of
like snail-slime.

I could lie and say the thing
grossed me out too – ok, it
did a tiny bit, but not much.

Truth is the sight of it pierced me
with keen pleasure. Joy, even.
I couldn't help but smile.
I might have laughed
out loud, but I'm generally
not that type.

If we were working on a metaphor here,
this might spell trouble.
(see stanza one)

But no –
somewhere there's a woman
loose in town
spreading the truth about me.

Is it possible, I ask you,
to start a day
any better than that?

Big honkin' loogie!

(See stanza one)

Children Left in the Palm of Your Hand

Sometimes it can be too slow in coming.
Maybe the movement is wrong. Perhaps
It's the time. So many years for it all
To swim through. Can Passion make it out
Of a past like that into the present?
If it doesn't make it out, I say it can't
Be passion. And if it does, I say
The mind will open to it as easily as eager lips.

From that opening it's a long way to here,
To this page, or this life. They say
So much dies on the way. But sometimes
I still feel it. A shudder will starts inside
After the opening. It will tease up old responses,
Loosen all that has tried to dry up. Then
Everything will flow easily. And what it was
Will move deeper into what I remember now.

I can't say it feels the same. I can't
Say I don't know what is happening. I can't
Even warn you, like I would then, that it's
Coming, it's coming! But I will tell you this,
Dear. After all the years of separation
It carries everything we gave back then.
And I will tell you this too. Those children
I left in the palm of your hand come alive,
They come alive, love, they come alive.

Cape Sounion

Byron: your name as simple as that
Still lies chiseled into the flat column
At Sounion. Today I climbed ancient
Steps to trace the letters. Don't be fooled.
This wasn't easy. Call it an effort of faith.
Diplomacy and clever phrasing, hollow promises
And lies were tendered like offerings to Poseidon.

She would have none of it.
She was tired of the Greeks and the heat.
She was giving herself away through the pores
And said something was missing. Each day she
Ran in unfashionable streaks to the ground.
Gray stains bloomed under her arms, on her back.

She carried water in a plastic jug.
It wasn't enough. Now she has left me
For the Aegean. She wants it all
And won't listen. She opens her mouth
At its shore. She gulps and cries at once.
You must know how that is. Today I turned to you.
I put one dry finger in the smooth groove
And slowly and delicately traced your name.

Syrup

Think you've been lonely
try sub-B movie in boondocks Utah
TV broken cheap motel
weeks on the road no conversation

Try finding a seat next to a knockout woman
& you're so lonely so horny &
can't tell which & don't care & can't
find words to say witty suave something
to hide the soul & force a smile

Try sweaty palms on the armrest
& it seems forever you're on the verge
of saying what you don't know & so don't
in fact except the thousand dialogues
stuttering inside the skull

Try getting carried away in that skull
thinking if she spoke your life would change
& how she could save you
from the road madness that strands
you town after town in bad movies

Then try keeping it all together
when he shows up younger than you
but hard to tell teeth like quartz
tall big shoulders washboard abs no doubt
& box of unbuttered in each hand

Try swallowing the smile she gives you
before lights go out giving her
back one of your own opening wide
eyes saying all right no harm

Try sitting through the whole movie
while she hogs the armrest &
your feet stuck in syrup that won't let go

Trains and Philosophy

The train is
late
getting to
Flagstaff.

Old guy on
the bench
tells me he likes
chicks with
dicks videos.

He always wanted
to have
one, see what
it's like.

Truth is,
he says, have you
ever seen
them, they're
really not good
looking, not that
good, anyway.

That's too
bad,
I say.

But now the
Pope,
he says, the
Pope's

the one. I
blame him.
He hasn't called
me in weeks,
though.

A new
announcement
says the
train, for a reason
nobody understands,
will be
even later.

Chicks with
dicks and
the Pope.

Go on old
man,
I say,
I'm listening.

The Nymphomaniac

Every guy I knew wanted her.
Even too young to know what it was about,
I would find her latest number to dial
Away at the urges I couldn't understand,
Encouraged by the label
Everyone knew meant you could say or do
Anything you wanted and she wouldn't care.

I remember a hot night one summer
Walking home at a deep hour
And the intentional detour through the alley
Behind her house, the latest radio music
Barely audible behind the quiet window light
Where I imagined her naked and eager
And wondered if *anything you want*ed
Included everything I had heard of,
Or was there more?

Anything you wanted. Another way of saying
Other guys had already done it.
Another way of saying I didn't know what
It was, but I could do it too,
And more if I had the courage. Another way
Of saying no one sat next to her
In class, even guys I knew she had done
Anything they wanted with. Another way
Of saying no one ever took her
To a dance, no one ever met her parents.

Where did she go? She's only a face now,
One that disappears suddenly from the yearbooks.
I remember how the rumors lived on

After she moved, how those rumors grew
year by year breeding their own kind until
Anything you wanted became everything she had been.

When I find her last photo in a line-up
Of classmates, I discover a face
More eloquent in its flat silence
Than all the stories.
One look at the eyes tells me that her smile was a lie.
I imagined that same dark stare
In hundreds of forgotten yearbooks
Accusing only the darkness of the page shut against it.
And I see myself again
On that summer vigil
Lurking at the edge of the truth,
Hearing the fuzzy static from a tiny transistor radio
Held hopefully to her ear,
Songs that could never drown out the voices crying
Anything you wanted
That must have pounded inside her like fists.

The Pod

Woman & you finally get together –
her place, dinner.
Little tyke in bed early.
Chit chat, good grub & all,
the whole shebang moving nicely
toward some pleasurable nexus.
Until sometime later she beckons,
and you follow her down the hall,
enjoying here a bit of masculine
norm, incipient tumescence.
She leads you into a room,
& before you know it
she's saying look, her face
agleam & the screen starting to glow
like virtual interruptus
at mega digit megahertz or something,
her voice giddy with acronyms,
all that clicking & clacking
filling up the space between you.
Down the hall the child turns
in sleep, his sigh smothered by
clacking too & she's naming people
she's connected to now & rooms
that she joins or something,
& all the aliases she uses so
they don't really know who she is.
She keeps saying if only
you'd get one too then you could
communicate whenever & really
get to know each other &
the whole time she never looks
away from the screen, the slight blush

you notice below the collarbones
keeping you going but thinking
now it might be her Chardonnay &
when she describes her mouse, you
want to say that it's probably
the only thing her pussy wants, but
you don't. You just watch her face
watching the screen, & when you hear
the kid again, you glance down the hall
& suddenly it's like a tunnel,
a scene from the old black and white
classic, "Invasion of The Body Snatchers,"
& the paranoia of Kevin McCarthy
spreading through you & you start
to realize how her face reflected on
the screen reminds you of Dana Wynter,
& you're afraid any moment now she'll
turn to you sweetly, blanks in her eyes,
& tell you how easy it all is,
how wonderful.

The Black Poem

I was showing
a much younger
woman
The White Album.
By the
Beatles, of
course.

Here it
is, The
White Album,
I said.

She held it
in her hands,
looked
it over,
intrigued.

Then she took
out the vinyl
and her
face soured
over.

This is
black,
she said,
holding
the vinyl up
to show me.

It isn't
white,
she said.

What could
I say?

Maybe they
meant
the album cover,
I said.
The White
Album Cover.

But it was too late –
a matter of trust,
perhaps.

Whatever,
that night
her vinyl did not
make it
to the turntable.

COFFEE

Say it's a donut shop in a strip mall.
Say a young guy comes in because his buddy
needed a cup of coffee. Say the guy's good
looking – tall, dark curly hair, eyes that could
melt a young girl's heart, a heart like
the one beating faster now in the girl behind
the counter. Say the guy starts to flirt
with the girl, just to impress his buddy.
Pretty soon what you have going are two
lives becoming one. Two lives giddy
and lustful in the beginning. Two lives
fucking like mad wherever and whenever
they can. Thinking they have it made.
Thinking no one's ever done what they're
doing or felt like they're feeling. Finding
out the truth real soon but finding it out too late.
Say they have a child. Then another. Say
there's never enough money. Everything
they need is something they can't afford.
Of course these lives will turn on each other.
Eventually, naturally, it will turn real ugly –
just another pitiful tale of misery ending with debris.
Before that, before the buddy needed coffee,
there was no donut shop in the strip mall.
But somebody got in touch with somebody.
Demographics were studied. Business
was conducted and eventually the place caught
on. It's a good location, right on the corner
of busy streets. The owner hires a young girl,
too young, he thinks. But the girl works out.
Everything looks good. The girl is happy.
It's her first job. She's making her own money.

She thinks this could be the first step to something.
Then, somewhere miles away from all this
a guy's buddy stays out all night for no good reason.
He tells the guy riding shotgun to look
for some place he can get coffee. He needs
coffee real bad. He won't make it otherwise.
The guy riding shotgun looks out the window.
Maybe it's raining slightly that morning.
Or maybe there's a bit of fog. Who remembers?
But the guy riding shotgun sees a sign right off.
There's a donut shop, he says. Good, says the driver.

Sunset in Shades of Desire

Clouds clotting up a pastel sky & some kind
of sunset on the way as you leave
the car the potpourri of license plates &
head for the sand dunes folded
up out of Death Valley –
like a blanket rumpling the desert she says
or like a sandy sea in storm you say
& on you go swapping images
like ripples in bad paint
or quickspread icing on dry cake
like dirty clouds dropped from the sky
she says & all the time
you imagine them to yourself
giant pink labias in sunset moistened by rare rain
& you're still lovers at this point
hand in hand & you think you see a bastion
a quiet vantage where you might shed
a garment or two & fold each other into
grains of love & share the sunset
& you're about to say so but something
goes tweak in her harmonic convergence maybe
who knows but she's gone already
giving herself up to tourist simplicities
& suddenly you have no choice she having
scuttled up the nearest dune &
tumbled out of sight into a chasm of herself
& what is there now
except the tallest dune & a solo ascent
the slope all granular trudging and no hand to seek
no oasis of shared breathing
only sand filling shoes & churning thighs
& hellacious sweat & someday you'll have to

remember it all just like this –
yourself climbing the world's tallest labia
& the sun turning everything pink &
not going anyplace only the sensation
of sinking deeper & deeper despite the effort
& no erection anywhere on the horizon

Two Lattes

Up against it yes once again –
there she is two lattes to go which makes you wonder

She kept her number but took your heart
dropped what was left of you
into her purse no change & a loud snap
that old fashioned clasp like handcuffs for your balls
& no key anywhere

She's moving fast her two lattes & tight jeans
through the door already & she's
on the sidewalk before you hear the slow voice
she left behind for your listening pleasure.

Seems she wasn't ready for another relationship
seems the last one drank
and beat her not at first of course but then regular
seems she's just not ready you understand

Hell yes of course naturally you understand
the two lattes to go which still make you
wonder tight jeans nice ass
which you didn't say right out given
the circumstances but hell yes you understand

It's simple understand: another asshole
somewhere bottle in one hand sickness in the other
just kicked you long distance
in the balls & the two lattes to go which
still makes you think are now
a brake light at the corner & then gone: gone

Slo-Pitch in Chinook, Washington

One team keeps going round and round
Running up a score that was lopsided
Before you arrived. They're playing under
A tough sky – so gray and blank every fly
Loses identity and disappears. The women,
Drunk and pale in the tiny stands, ride
Their men hard. They've forgiven too much
At home to overlook the errors committed here.
You identify with the men. You've been
Out in that field yourself and you know it's
The sky. You'd like to tell the outfielders that
It's just a matter of the weather, nothing more.
Under different clouds the women would cheer.

But this is an old game and everybody knows
The rules. Until it rains that sky is only a place
For the flies to get lost in. Those women know it,
And their love shows the count on every pitch.
They know the fielder's blank faces mean nothing.
Even the score out here isn't the issue anymore.
You've been at bat in this game too. That's why you
Leave before the inning is over. It's why you take
The quick path back to a safe campground. You know
That unless the pitcher starts to find the corners
Or that unfaithful sky begins to clear overhead,
The balls of those cold fielders will hang out there
All night just as empty as scoreboard zeroes.

Separate Rooms

Every wall seems flat and moves
to a corner we want no part of.
This room, like the short time spent
together – one bed, small closet,
chair and dresser, one way out,
the way we came in. Each evening
bringing the old day back to the same
address with us, setting what
we could understand on the dresser –
a few misunderstandings, the lovers left
behind, a future we kept looking
for, everything we were afraid
to say to each other. We never
mentioned money, never asked
what it takes to keep something
like this together. It didn't take
long before it all started getting
smaller than we would have predicted,
before there was too much
light coming through the window,
before the dust everywhere became
an issue, before our only intimacy
became the corners, those promises
we forced each other into.
When the rent came due it didn't
take long – one of us promised to turn
out the lights, and the other would
lock the door, both of us leaving with
the keys we once accepted but would
never return. Sort of like the love.

The Gym for Settling Old Scores

It's an old game you've been playing forever.
A scoreboard that won't lie says you're losing –
Playing catch up against a team with more talent
And no mercy. They're taller and quicker than
You are. One gets free and dunks so hard you duck
As the ball explodes through the net. Fans go wild.

It's happening in front of the whole town.
A big game. Everyone you know has traveled
All the way here to watch. The crowd keeps yelling
No matter what the score, and the cheerleaders
Won't let them stop. This game goes way back –
You remember them scrubbed, modest breasts
Under bulky blue sweaters – cheerleaders who
Would never let you quit. You still don't know
Why the one you wanted never looked your way.

The referees always gave you trouble. Their shirts
Were black and white, and that's the way they
Saw everything. Their whistles made a sound
That you expected to hear the rest of your life.
During timeout a cheerleader screams your name.
Her mouth is hard, lipstick smeared, mascara
Etched into the old lines you can never avoid.
She leaps and her legs spread for the crowd.

This is the only game whose rules you haven't forgotten.
You try making all the old moves, ones that worked
Years ago. But the coach you always hated still screams
Your name with a voice that's followed you everywhere.
Every time the whistle blows the crowd shouts your number,
And another old lover goes to the line to shoot two.

What's Forgotten, What's Not

Her face,
even, has faded.
The taste
of her?
The smell?
I can't say.

But I recall
that in 1911
John Browning
gave us
the M1911
.45 automatic
pistol.

Later known as
the M1911A1,
it fired a
230 grain,
fully jacketed
bullet.

Velocity 850 ft.
per second,
approximately, giving
it 350 foot pounds
of energy
on impact,
approximately.

She was tall,
or so
I think.
But her breasts?
The color
of her hair?

All that
disappeared
somewhere.

But I remember
that the .45 I
owned
when I knew
her had
checkered grips,
mahogany –
the color of
her eyes,
perhaps.

When I pulled
the trigger,
that .45 bucked
like something
wild in
my hands.

So did she.

Now that I
think
of it.

The Women on Rhodes

It's while holding your penis cold and limp
Swaying in the hotel bathroom on Rhodes
That you feel the fever come on inside you.
Sweat pops from your forehead like hammered
Chips must have sprung from those statues
You've admired all through this country.
Soon you're burning up and know it's serious.
You hold on to the cold limp penis for life,
And it seems to urinate out of ancient grief.

You try to keep everything under control.
You gulp down gallons but water runs through
You so fast it splashes out contempt
For the searing tissues that must scream
For it. Outside it's dark. There's a disco
In a park across the street. Another mistake.
The music is American, the voices European.
You're not sure, maybe French maybe Scandinavian,
But women so pleased to be where they are
They can't help being too happy, too loud.
The penis you hold grows silent and angry.

It keeps shrinking into you. It wants no part
Of this. And your testicles drop away too.
A tactical move to protect sperm from fevers,
You recall from somewhere. They knew before you
That hamburger was bad. All night you soak
Through sheets on two beds. You chew aspirin
Like peanuts and clutch again and again
The only part of you that knows what to do.

And always those voices. In languages you don't
Speak the meaning gets louder – they're so glad
To be here, they've never had so much fun.

Maybe you forgive them now. But you're not sure.
In the morning you walked to Mandraki Harbor
And sipped cup after cup of tea. You ate
Scraps of toast, read the *Herald Tribune*.
You studied the women too. Noticed how
They looked without the silk and makeup
That the dreams in your dark fever gave them.
It all happened many years ago and you still
Remember how thankful you were for the sweet
Tea and dry toast that stayed in your stomach.

But it's still not that simple. You can appreciate
The shrewd biology that knew when to drop
Your fragile sperm away from the dangerous heat
Of your sickness. But forgiveness? That takes
A lot more than biology. Earlier you said maybe.
You're still trying to decide. It's a question
You continue to straddle – straddle with your
Feet planted firmly on the shores of resentful memory,
The tide between your legs going in, going out.

OLD SAGE & THE BITCH

Once your car broke down
place called Wagon Mound, New Mexico
a desperate situation
you & a young woman
with no money to speak of
& you with a life that already broke down
in the place you left
& the woman
hoping for a new life
in a place she'd never been

'63 Chevy losing power
hacking smoke
out the exhaust
trunk & back seat stuffed with everything
you had to drag with you
the weight of it all
finally too much for the Chevy

Pulled into a Texaco
& the old guy stepped from a service bay
dark rage of his native forefathers
still in the eyes
you & the young woman feeling
real white & helpless

Hardly said a word
barely a glance at your woman
lifted the hood & went at it
with rags & the tools he carried
pulled a screwdriver from a back pocket
popped the distributor cap

& tinkered
singing all the while
to himself
finally said, try it
& you did & the straight six
hummed smooth as the prairies
you'd been crossing
for days

He pulled a rag & wiped his hands
the afternoon breeze lifting the ponytail
off his back
shook his head
as he refused your money &
said nothing was broke
things just needed some adjustment

That was it
quick thanks a wave & you were off
when the young woman shifted
gears the old heap surged
like a stallion & you studied her face
there was a lot of road
ahead of you & you wondered
how many miles her frown could last

The Point

She's at the kitchen table
& he's stretched on the couch &
it hasn't been a good day something
more than they bargained for
having drifted between them that morning
& it won't leave &
she's supposed to be working &
he's pretending to read
& he can hear her laptop clacking
out line after line & all
he has is a stubby pencil #2 Ticonderoga
& book margins hardly a match
& he's doing the best he can whenever
she pauses scratching out his
own line take that touché sort of &
it's not easy the point
going fast on his Ticonderoga & her
showing no signs of letting up
& unless he's mistaken
not a sharpener in the whole house

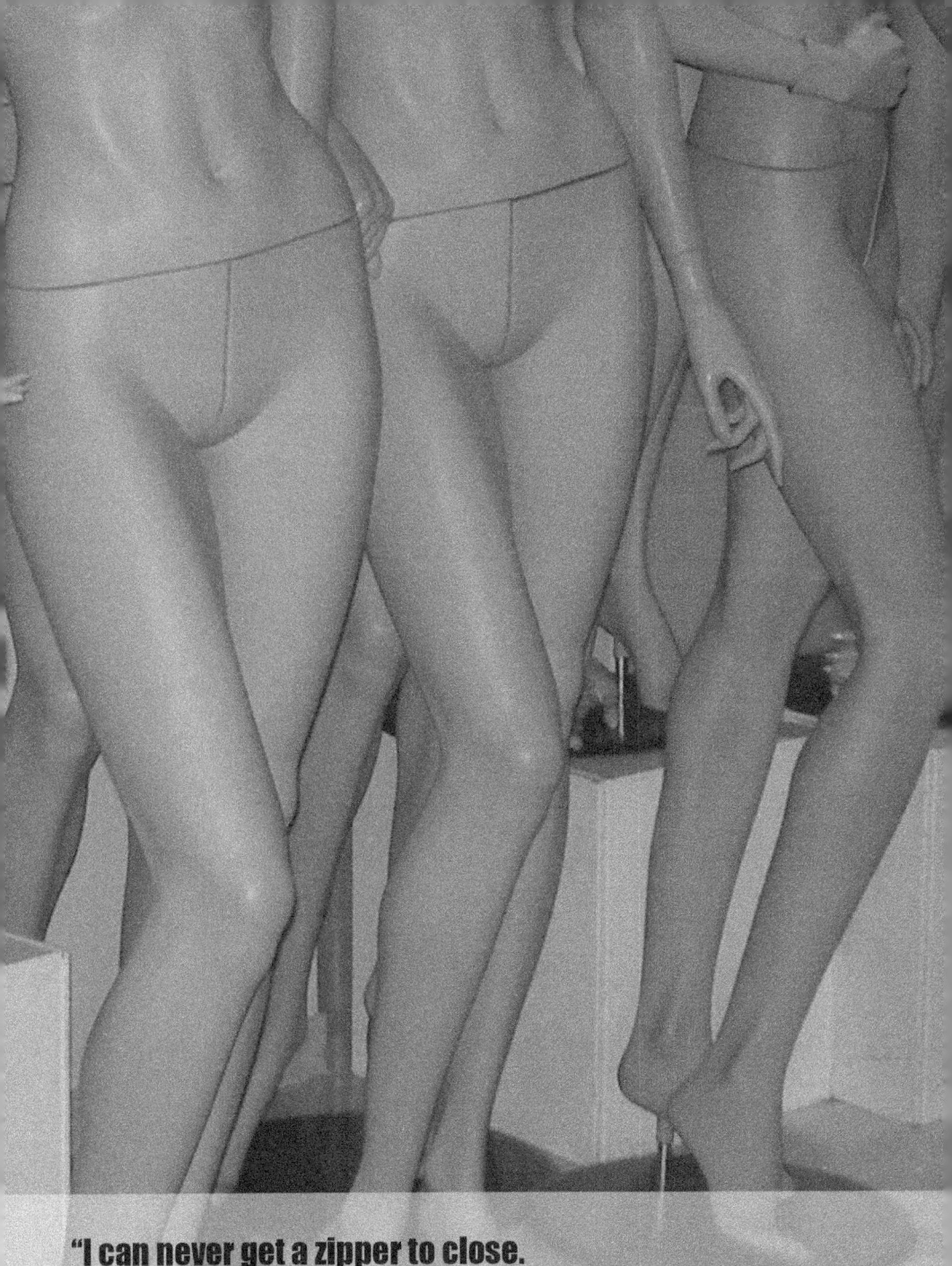

"I can never get a zipper to close.
Maybe that stands for something. What do you think?"
Rita Hayworth, *Gilda*

Laundry

If you could find the moves again or remember
The sweet phrases that once pleased, here
Before the tumbling machines in the dense
Swelter of damp clothes and dryer-heated air,
What would happen? She's changed
After all these years. Arms shaking the static
Out of slips are loose in the triceps.
She bends at a waist that refuses the bending.
Thighs she once guarded seem relieved
Of modesty and made peace with a gravity
They can't fight anymore. In her basket
Lies a life she's still hoping to keep clean –
Tiny socks wadded by heat, colorful blouses,
And nylon lumps unfolded into sexy shapes.

It's from a sorting table that you watch her –
Peering over the top of the morning newspaper.
You could leave. Escape to the coffee shop.
Nothing to worry you there except the imagination
And all those different paths your lives won't take –
Friends you won't pester for rumors, how they
Tempt you with all the latest. That she remembers
How good you were together, wants another shot at it.
That you dine, make love again. How you're sensitive
To the stretch marks and skin that betrayed her.
The way you strum her belly like a washboard,
Hum ditties, make her laugh like before. Speaking
Of the old times with affection, recent times
With dismay, and the future with fresh hope . . .

When you lower the paper, she's already gone.
Two brats scream for attention. A tired mama

Screams back for respect. There's too much heat
Spilling out of the dryers and someone's dumped
Your clothes in a basket. Picking them up,
One by one, shaking them out, you think of her –
Her hands – how they could still teach you a thing
Or two about laundry: the way all the old lives
should be cleaned, folded, then put neatly away.

PHONES

There's a pay phone still ringing somewhere inside the old world.
It's right there on the corner.
Some nights I imagine that it never stops and lights
go on all over the place and pissed off tax payers
with pillow hair lean out their windows and threaten each other.
This has nothing to do with ring tones.
This is serious.
I was seven when we got our first phone. We had a party line.
Our ring was two shorts and I screwed up once
and answered two long rings, which was the Ramsey's across the
    alley.
I laid the phone on the table and ran over to the Ramsey's
and banged on their door but they weren't home.
I knew I'd screwed up so I ran down the alley to Phil's house
and we read Comics
until his mom called my house to let my parents
know I was staying for dinner. Another time I spent a summer
living at the Bellevue Apartments in a phoneless room
with a Murphy bed. My girlfriend in the next town
would dial the phone booth at a gas station across the street.
Sometimes she called late, two or three in the morning.
That was when I really started to understand
life because I would lie in bed and taunt myself with
the image of someone else answering. Yes, someone else
getting there before me and stepping into my life and really all they
    had to do
was pick up the phone, you see,
and from there it would only be a matter of proper etiquette.
You must understand: it wasn't our phone and it never left the booth.
One night I waited all night and the phone never rang.
So the next night when it rang I didn't answer. It was eerie, let's be
    honest.

It rang all night and people kept picking up the receiver.
I watched them. They would look around.
They always looked around and they always shook their head. I liked that.
We broke up soon afterwards. We actually screamed
at each other about the phone,
but not over the phone.
The phone was black. It hung on a silver hook, and I had to push coins into
a slot if I called her. I wonder what happened to it.
We screamed at each other.
I had never screamed at another person like that before.

Marmaris Cafe

An old café on the waterfront of Marmaris.
Ramadan's over and every place
Looks flush, loud and ready for more.

The woman tells him she's boring

Then quickly turns her head and tries to smile,
The squeaking fan overhead
Lifting her incorrect tense onto the damp terrace.

Someone says it's the first rain in six months

And she smiles, and he frowns,
Unable to understand what was said –
The rain slashing at the roof

Being the only sound that makes sense to him.

He asks her a hybrid question complete with gestures.
She cocks her head and shrugs.
They lean into the table, faces nearly touching.

There's something they each want to say.
Something to penetrate the garlic each of them
Fears their words might become.

Before either one speaks,
One of them wonders if this is how wars begin.

Flash

Many years ago I slept in a bunk on an overnight train bound for
    Istanbul.

Once, when I awoke, I was told I was looking at Sofia,
Capital of Commie Bulgaria.
Then thunder rolled into our compartment searching for the lightning
That was last observed striking its allegiance in the hills
Above the city.

It wasn't lightning at all, really.
It was that cheap stuff you would see putting on a show for the masses
Or reflected in a woman's eye,

Perhaps,
Like in Belgrade – the fear then, yes, fear,

That would flash
In the eye that caught yours as the two of you passed each other
In Terazije Square –

The possibilities! Infinite, they would seem, for a moment,
Until the thunder.

Bound for Athens

The darkness beginning to ripen, to *expect*.
The ship splitting the sea into pleasures around us.

These are the moments that repeat.
That occur through sequencing memory and desire,
Concessions to need, ambivalent design
Of the clothing: the undressing after dressing.

The rustlings, the snaps and swishes.
Whisperings of release surrendering to uncertainties.
The untethering and unshrouding cloth.
Unwhispering. Making no comment.

That woman
On the ship to Athens, finger crooking to beckon
And the singular moment beginning to happen. Spawning
The deliberate and knowing of

Intentions. *How it discovers*: all the memories collected
Together, the smaller moments shuffled, dealt out, both

Playing the hand. A bare foot rising from the floor.
Something continuing
To unfold, the moments starting to be put in line.
One toe catching the falling lace,
Creating the instant in its drop to the floor.

A new buoyancy in the moment and the delight of premonition.
Mere ounces of sheerness
                popping up and down the blood.

And the encountering: something new along the arteries,

A manifesto of that moment: desire in flight
Through thin braided webs, flushing.
Let me tell you what I want, she says. Let me tell

You what will happen.
                    I speak your language,
She says. I know what should happen.
Tiny bumps in the areolas under her fingers rising.
That moment unshuffling from her hands, the tiny bumps
Still part of the sequence, what moves through her
Cabin while the ship rolls side to side, the tiny
Bumps tasting of salt, all of it churning in a wake
Of memory:

When this is over, she says, you must take me
On deck
And cast me into the sea.

Arrows

You're out with your dad's truck
and no license yet
keeping it on the dirt roads
and you come across a Corvair
stuck axle-deep
in the sandy wash below Crow Canyon,
fresh mounds of spun sand
piled behind the tires.
The marine flagged you down,
said, I'm AWOL in three hours man,
you gotta shovel ... can you help us?
He was stripped to the waist
smeared with the paste
of dirt and sweat, panic starting
to take over.
You two dug with bare hands
jacking the engine-heavy rear end
over and over, jamming rocks
under the tires, and each time the Corvair
lurched ahead five feet,
ten feet.

The whole time she
stretched out on the blanket
naked except for panties,
younger than you, maybe,
paying no attention to you or the marine,
taking her time with a cigarette,
the way she looked
making you sweat more than the Corvair.
Finally, you and the marine
got lucky.

The Corvair jumped from the mire,
found a hard patch
and slithered onto the road,
the marine jumping out
dropping one arm over your shoulder
all the panic gone,
saying baby whyn't you suck this guy
off real quick so we can go.
And you trying to say no, trying
to get out of it,
conscious of the sweat, the dirt slicked
into every pore.
And the marine just laughing
saying shit man she's good at it.
And her leading you behind
a bush saying, it ain't gonna hurt,
and of course it didn't.
Afterwards her face glancing up
from your belt buckle,
a sweet frown,
pupils blown open like balloons.

Years passed after that.
Until the night before your pre-induction
physical for the draft,
downtown LA, raising hell
with hometown buddies, one fight
already – Eddie jacking
a guy up against the wall in the hotel
screaming, what you looking
at asshole?
Finding a theater to cool down in
and finding her again –
not in person, a fake name in the credits,
her face, though, swallowing
the screen,

pimple tracks up the arms
and still good at it.
Working two cocks and a champagne bottle,
all three making a big splash,
licking champagne and come to the last drop.
Your buddies hooting
at the screen like it was the Three Stooges.

After that almost nothing for years,
decades even,
maybe a rumor now and then,
stuff you wouldn't repeat
even in something like this.
And somewhere in this stretch you read
about the 'arrow of time'
all physics, so direct so dependable,
always going where it should.
And you think, if only life
could fly as true, if you could
stop yourself
from tearing the feathers, bending the shaft
whatever it is
that makes the years miss their targets.

Time, you begin to understand, makes no judgment,
just gives us the space to make our own.
When you see her again,
it's been so long
you can't place the face, and no wonder –
it's a special homecoming,
decades of alumnae overflowing the town,
memories confused
by the aging realities, all those arrows
and the strange targets
they found.
And besides, she's camouflaged

with children, a boy her own height,
a girl up to her waist she can't stop hugging.

It comes back to you that night
at the dance,
watching her move with ease
through the throng, abstemious, cheerful,
on target even.
Every so often she looks your way,
not exactly at you,
though you're not sure – all those torn feathers
and missed opportunities
hindering your aim.
It goes on like that all night –
fleeting eye contact
and neither of you moving.
And each time it happens,
at each glance, you nock new determination
onto the worn string of guilt,
unable to draw it back, unable to give
yourself flight across the floor,
to put out your hand,
and ask her, simply, to dance.

Red '59 Ford Pickup

Up before the crack &
in the shower the mind
revs it up in reverse
& you see yourself behind the wheel
of that red '59 Ford pickup
& it's only been a few hours
since you & the old man dropped
a 390 into it the 390 coming
from Buddy Sims' '63 Galaxy
too many Coors & a sharp curve
putting the undamaged engine
up for sale

The old man said baby it a while
clutch & tranny may not be up to the muscle
& by that afternoon you've shut down
a 327 Impala & 289 4-barrel Mustang
the damn truck just screaming
down the quarter mile, granite boulders
in the bed keeping wheel hop
down getting off the line & this guy

Slips a twenty under the wiper blade
& you're off again & you got
him through first & catch a glimpse
off to the side & it's her legs
damn near hood length that get you –
nearly down to the bumper
on David's '55 Nomad & it's her all right
back in town for the summer
you guess but don't have time to dwell

Never making it into third, just a bunch
of gears screaming & yeah something burning
& that Chevy & twenty bucks blowing
right by you & you know it's the clutch &
coast it to the shoulder
thinking you got two things to consider

A clutch & old man you can't do nothing about
& her in the rearview jogging all smiles
& legs right up to her neck it seems
& you're calculating that with a beefed clutch
& a smile like that & them legs
summer could be the ride of a lifetime
& you gotta remind her again that it was
& still is when she wakes up

Godpowers & Choice

Where would you stop it – time that is
given godpowers & choice –
perhaps there where the air was cool
& smelled of fresh cut grass
& it was the bottom of the fifth maybe sixth
& the Bend Bucks minor leaguers
of no distinction were crushing the ball all over
their charming little park

& the sun was down & the lights
had just come on
& the five year old was beside himself with joy
fair or foul safe or out it made
no difference he jumped & shrieked all of it magic

& in your lap the three year old asleep
next to his mother
her body in a rare thaw her countenance
unfrowned for once & his slow breath

dribbling onto your shoulder
those tiny hands gripping one finger like a bat
& you thinking you had finally
parked one yourself swinging from the heels
bases loaded

Quality Time

After a while
she stopped
quivering
and
dropped the knife
into
my hand. I
took it
and slid it
back into the
wooden block
with
the other knives.

I was
about to
say
something.

Suddenly,
the children burst
in from
the backyard,
flushed
and dusty
with joy.

We need
something to
drink,
they said.

I poured
them
lemonade, and
they slurped
from mugs
shaped like
Disney characters.
We joined
them
at the table.

The children smiled
and we
smiled back.
For a moment,
we might
have
passed for
a family.

"Doesn't it ever enter a man's head that a woman can do without him?"

Ida Lupino, *Road House*

The Tongue and the Blonde

The tongue came out at the Plough,
a pub, down the street from the British Museum.
The blonde liked its sign, the stars, the Big Dipper.

The tongue liked that she was a blonde,
liked that she spoke Russian,
that she spoke comfortably of Marx and Lenin.

The tongue also wanted to speak. It waited
for its turn, and lay silently on the small round table
licking the blonde's glass of Guinness.

The conversation carried them to the new year,
yet the tongue held back, letting the minds
speak their minds.

But when they kissed in the year among the thousands
at Trafalgar, it was the tongue
that took her hand, that led her to the underground.

It was the tongue that tried to speak
on the long ride to her hotel,
for it was the tongue that had tired of the minds

speaking their minds, that now wished to say
to the blonde who spoke Russian
open your thighs for me, just once, tonight,
and I will say everything that was left unspoken.

A Prayer for Nikos Kazantzakis

I was here twenty-six years ago. I promised
myself that I would return, and here I am.
Nothing has changed and everything is different.
Right now I'm wondering about that cross.
The same wood as twenty-six years ago –
Or no? Personally, it looks just the same.
I'll stick with that. You still have the view,
I'll give you that much: location, location,
location, especially in death – especially then.
I brought a wife this time. That's right, despite
Zorba – the whole catastrophe, etc. She was
insistent. Had to see your grave. She's a big
fan, you see. And – glory be to all the dead gods –
she's fallen in love with Crete! Before we leave,
I'll have to take another photo of your epitaph.
For years I kept a framed photo of it on my desk:
"I hope for nothing; I fear nothing; I am free."
Easy for you to say, as they say, but no less true.
I tried, certainly, but the world has a way of poking
its global nose into life . . . but let's not go there.
No, here's the truth: This isn't really a prayer.
Praying is for the insane. This is better. It's advice.
Lie still, old man. Stay quiet. It isn't safe yet.
There's still too much madness everywhere.

Pantoum of Sex

The bed, of course, is the map.
Everyone is looking for directions,
Folding and unfolding the sheets,
Wondering is this north or south.

Everyone is looking for directions.
Trying to find the best way there,
Wondering is this north or south,
Estimating their time of arrival.

Trying to find the best way there,
Everyone discovers their favorite route.
Estimating their time of arrival,
Wondering if they'll come early or late.

Everyone discovers their favorite route.
Hoping they don't make a wrong turn,
Wondering if they'll come early or late,
Always concerned about the traffic.

Hoping they don't make a wrong turn,
Folding and unfolding the sheets,
Always concerned about the traffic.
The bed, of course, is the map.

Toasting the Monsters

Remember this, old buddy, when
all else fails.
When the road madness – yeah,
two lane blacktop fever –
when that drives you too far from
what you most desire.

Remember this: Montreux, Switzerland.
Remember?
Coffee end of a good lunch.
Next to the lake. Those
big clouds across the lake, black
and pulpy and spitting lightning.

Until, finally, the clouds
dumped on us and we took shelter
inside? Remember?

We had given up women. Again.
Vowed never. Again.
Too damned much trouble. That was it!
Again. Of course.

And the Villa Diodati. How we
stood at the ferry's railing
that morning. Gliding along.
Water just a whisper on the hull below.
The best kind of quiet.

Then the speaker overhead telling us all
about Lord Byron, Percy and Mary Shelley.

And you said, "Women sure have a knack
for creating monsters."

Just off-hand. A casual comment.
But I still hear it, old buddy!
Like the loud crack of a christening
smashing into the hull
of all the future regrets. Carbonated truth
splashing over everything.

Once inside, you proposed a toast.
We raised glasses. Clinked.
Big plate glass windows all around
getting battered like hell by the storm.
"To the monsters," one of us said.
We had to laugh.
And so we did. Now, let me propose it
again – to the monsters! Yes, once again,
old buddy. To the monsters!

Every Good Story

Every good story starts on the balcony of a tropical hotel
With a view of the Pacific Ocean.
Maybe it's not the Pacific Ocean, but it's an ocean all right,
Or at least a major sea,
Visible beyond all the palm trees and swaying masts in the harbor.
Every good story has a ceiling fan turning overhead
Even if the air's too thick and it feels nicer on the balcony.
If it's still a good story, the guy on the balcony
Doesn't want any bizarre shit
To happen – he's too old now for anything that
Isn't soft and witty, with advanced degrees in philosophy.
He wants her to read philosophy
To him on the balcony – she can stay on the bed
Even, it doesn't matter.
If the guy is lucky her first language isn't English
And she hates America,
Has no desire to ever go to America, its corporate militarism makes
Her want to puke, you hear me, shush,
Jesus, they'll hear you all the way back in Virginia somewhere.
She always wants to know if he's CIA,
And he tells her every time that everybody is CIA, that's how bad it is.

Torture me then, she says, but she's smiling, and besides every good
Story gets rid of America as soon as possible.
In fact this story is so good that America won't come up again –
Unless it invades this story or something.
She likes throwing her hair back and propping her feet on the balcony
Next to his. In fact, they both like it.
Tonight she has a real treat for him – that's what she says, a real treat,
And he likes the way she says it – a real treat.
The way she says it tells him she must mean beyond post modernism,
    at least.

You see, he's at that point now,
A point in life he never even knew existed before,
That point where he finally has the balcony he always wanted,
One with at least two big French doors that
Open on different sides of the room so he can avoid or pursue the sun,
Whatever, but a damn fine balcony where
Nobody who walks by on the street below wants to speak English
And she knows it's all right to open her book
At random, any page will be just fine, and she never has to ask
For permission to start reading.

Segues

One fine spring day the sun heats their local majestic mountains
Until a sort of epistemological chasm erupts through the campground

Exposing a fault line of disharmony.
There's big Richter numbers belching in the ground and only the
    swarming flies,
Pancake and syrup crazed,

Move without panic as the woman stomps to the tent, driven by the
    man's jesting,
The epicenter of her disgust.

And she wants to know.
Her grizzly voice demands to know, right now, goddamn you,

Why would the man ever come up with such an idea?

The man thinking that such ideas are merely spontaneous neural
    segues, dear,
Obscure cognitive links dressed up and thrust onstage

To let Hamlet know about the ghost.

Segues being the favorite stitch of that force knitting across intervals
    between
Life and past,
The man sees himself again in dusty Turkey, the little village near
    Ephesus,
The Hotel Aksoy, breakfast at the Café Artemis.

The nasty thing about segues is that flies understand them, too.
There was a plague of flies at the Artemis,

Everyone forced to eat face down, mouths tightened against the
    swarm.

Segues are not gender specific, and soon the needles of necessity knit
Ella back into the breakfast scene,
Lines of sweat like the long, swift thin tails of tiny creatures just
    missed
Streaking down her neck.

Look, there's not a single segue in the whole fucking world that would
    allow its
Stitch to be dropped here,
Not with Ella squeezing fresh mango juice sweetly over her neck and
    breasts,

Not with the way the flies applauded the gesture and instantly
    performed
A swift charge of the flight brigade.
Uh, uh,
Segues exist for the wink she gave him, for the naked pen and ink
    sketching
Done at the edge of the sea, for the way she tasted of mangoes in the
    morning,
For how she got away even before the man's Rhodes-bound ferry
Stretched the sea between them –

And, yes,
For women in their tents everywhere howling at all the jests, mangoes
    or no,
For sticky icky flies wherever they are,
And, mercifully, for those unexpected aftershocks that shake the mind
    loose
Without warning or reason.

Love's Passport

I

Security puts us through metal detectors again.
The machine thinks it knows all about me.
My wife asks, are you ok? Her life is cleared.
I remain a cause for alarm. Everyone sees it.
The x-ray woman frowns. Is it the keys?
Sir, step over here. Sir, step back please.

I raise my arms. I have become a reminder.
A dime for every prying eye. I'm ready to confess.
The x-ray woman takes my wife's hand.
She's sorry. My wife says, it's ok. Soon,
They'll find everything she suspected.
They won't even have to hurt me.

II

The room is too small in every country we visit.
It backs us into corners only the locals enjoy.
Cars honk outside like we're in the way.
We move the bed. A soccer ball caroms
into the room. A small intense face hovers
outside the window, three stories up.
Motions for the ball. Give him the ball,
my wife says. Like hell, I say.

I can still see that face at the window.
Deep, foreign shade of darkness, black
hair, waiting for the ball. His eyes mysterious
as dark matter. Putting me on trial
In the room, waiting for the ball, his ball.

This is his country. He will hover outside
the window as long as he damn well pleases.
And if he blinks, I know I might disappear.

III

No matter how tall it is, we will climb to its top.
The view is magnificent and disappointing.
We hurt. We huff, we puff. Long moments
staring. Regretting the effort, dripping, everything
sticking to us. Taking photos in every
disappointing direction, smiling, smiling.
Wondering, why the hell was it ever built?
Wondering, why the hell did we decide to climb it?

Knowing why as soon as we get down:
The stupid sense of accomplishment.
Having done it. Entitled to bore others with
The story of climbing it. Changing the story
Each time. Making it more beautiful, full
Of wonder. And no, not that hard really.
Making certain others will climb it and suffer too.

IV

Every cathedral is gigantic and old and must be seen.
But not believed, fortunately, since the old lies
Don't change. The weight of the structures dwarfed
Only by their weight of oppression, which is why
They compel people to look up – so people won't
Forget something is always looking down on them.
They're so magnificent, my wife dutifully says
To everyone near enough to hear her and smile.

Ah, but the pretty windows. Yes. One concedes
The beauty of stained glass, with or without blood.

Of course, there's a shit-load of history in cathedrals.
But then, everything abroad has a shit-load of history.
Every cathedral has its own particular interior hum.
Ever notice? Once, hoping to put a stop to the hum,
I stood in a corner and pressed my ear to the wall.
Didn't work. From within the wall came screams
From all the witches they burned. Well, maybe not *all*.

    V

Museums have the tallest ceilings in the world.
Unbelievable. I know all that vacant space overhead
Is supposed to be aesthetic, but someone please tell me why.
The hardest part is knowing how long you're supposed
To look at each work of art. How much time to take in each
Salon, etc. I can sprint until nudity is only about being naked,
Nothing about god. Then I idle back. I never go in
Salons with cherubs, and that's where I lose the wife.

Most of the museum cafes are better than the museum.
It's no contest. I'll get there hours before my wife.
She gets stuck in the Renaissance, where most of
The stuff is about floating or butchery. Museum cafes
Are about food on your own tray, a patio, reading.
People look at each other in the cafes. I know, here's
Where you expect the line that goes, after all, each of us
Is a work of art. But that's a lie. Hardly anyone is.

    VI

Every good vacation abroad includes a Greek island.
Guaranteed – it has an ancient site you must see. Never
Admit you missed an ancient site – Americans can't
Go to Greek islands anymore just to goof off. Man, they
Look so sad, walking in packs, staring at the ancient
Holes, nodding at the guide's every word. You know

They're all thinking about lunch and worried as hell
About the beach – all the topless broads, etc.

Without a doubt the best island in Greece is Crete.
Iraklion is heaven. Wife and I sit for hours in cafes
Near the harbor. After dinner we'll stroll through
The city. We'll sit on a bench near Kazantzakis'
Grave and whisper to each other. When the sun
Sets, my wife gives me this smile. Then she'll stand up,
Spread her arms wide, throw her head back and howl
Like a wolf in the hills. Man, talk about love.

The Cow Never Seen in a Photograph

A cow in the west of Ireland tires
of the grass it has been chewing and begins
to lumber into the next field
where fellow cows are grazing
and the grass has always appeared greener.

The passenger in a car driving past notices
the cow's movement, points out the window
and says, "Look, that's such a pretty cow."
So far, everyone's morning has gone quite well.

The driver of the car is thinking of his meds.
Taken out of synch with the monitored illness,
they seem to have run amok along
the various distribution routes of his neural/chemical
system. He doesn't want to look at cows.

"Let's stop," the passenger says, "I want to take
a picture." The driver's meds don't like this.
The road is too narrow, it has no shoulder,
and stone walls crowd both sides. "Not now,"
the driver says, "there will be other cows."

The cow, meanwhile, has nearly reached
the field that appears greener. The cow happens
to be a striking specimen of the breed known
as Irish Moiled. Its nutty brown hide is splashed
with a powdered sugar whiteness that extends
over its face, making it, indeed, quite photogenic.

Even before the cow reaches the greener field,
the mood inside the car has taken a turn for the worse.

Inside the head of the passenger is a synaptically
induced video wherein she sees herself boarding
a flight back to America, alone, free, triumphant.

In the small village of Roundstone the passenger
will walk by herself to the end of the stone jetty
all the while re-living and analyzing
her entire life down to the minutest details.
Before she reaches the end, she will quiver with rage.
She will stare out at the sea and ask the cosmic *why?*
The driver of the car, meanwhile, has discovered
a musical instrument shop not far from the jetty.
He appears to be fascinated by a window display
of handcrafted bodhrans. In fact, he is actually thinking
of "The Mackintosh Man," starring Paul Newman. Scenes
from that film, he has realized, were shot in the town.

It will be a long time before the driver and the passenger
again share the compact space of their rented car.
Before that ever happens, the cow will reach the greener
field and join other cows in their three-hour lunch of Ireland's
finest. There, it will eat methodically and contentedly
unaware that its photo was not and never will be taken.

FACES SING, AND LOUDER SING, AT THE REUNION

Everyone here has two faces – the face showing
the life it lives now
and a face the other faces remember from the past.
A rat has eaten one of the faces,
the face of someone called Jim
who tells me in a voice limp as the handshake
that he has cancer of the brain.
In his voice I hear the hymns of a funeral
that I will read about in a few months.

A man called George who was the boy called Rocky
greets me on the porch
in the air of an early morning too warm
for November. He talks of his own first death,
something he takes as much pain
to describe as it must have caused.
He spares nothing, pointing to where he says
the pus – like snot sort of (and he laughs) –
oozes from his abdomen into a bag.
He tells me of the coincidence that saved
his life, the nurse we both went to school with,
how she pulled him out of the bright globe
of a coma to hold his hand.

Inside, a DJ cues up more of those songs
that the faces we no longer have
still cling to. Now it's surf music – "Wipe-out," "Pipeline,"
hits from the lives we pretended to live
until the ones we couldn't avoid took hold for good.
In a woman's mouth I find myself seeking
the tongue of a virgin whose rejection once stung.
It's a kiss so desperate that it can't feel

all the years stacked up, like old '45's on spindles
of our past. And it can't silence the scratchy 'Goodies
being cued up by the lost loves, young rockers
who knew the music they fed us would never
stop, even when death started to sing in their grooves.

In the Sangre de Cristo Mountains

A cold stillness that even the morning's reverence
Of birds won't crack.

The mountains darkly poised
Beneath them
Ready to roll like waves onto the endless prairie beach.

It's a day larger than geography unwrapping from the earth.

Suddenly, she's had enough of this.
She's saying it's time to get back – she needs her coffee.

Couple more lines, he tells her.
I was just coming to grips with the vastness, etc.

Honey, she says,
I'm freezing, baby, and I don't have a clue about them birds not
Cracking stillness – did you mean silence?

Imagery, dear. I was capturing the awe, the majesty of our
created earth.

Like nobody's done that one before, she says.

A silent coldness
That even the irreverent birds can't pierce.

Honey, she says,
It's damn cold up here. It's pretty and all but can't you write it
Where it's warm?

In the cabin

They stand at the window and watch a raven shake down
A cascade of snow from its perch
While the fireplace next to them begins to roar
With flames of unholy beauty.

Honey, she says,
Look at that fire – write about that next time.

The Mohs Scale

The Jeep gets us deep into
the desert,
place full of nowhere,
the rugged solitude of a granite
canyon, sage, creosote,
unseen creatures
waiting for the night, ancient
heat,
chunks of bright quartz
flushed down
the canyon by geology
and those big forces of nature.

On the way I've been showing off,
pointing out
the fault line, a left-lateral
and dead, they say—classifying
the rocks, granite,
quartz, all the igneous,
the limestone, and the stretch of talc
off to the south
mined for decades before it
played out, the main
shaft still
visible – and the Mohs' scale,
I bring that up,
Friedrich Mohs, German, clever scale
for finding a mineral's
hardness, talc getting a one, diamond a ten,

all based upon whether
a mineral scratches or gets scratched
when rubbed against
another mineral.

We strip,
both of us slick from the heat,
blanket
crunchy on the sand and the sweat
keeps coming and she
starts a little foreplay, tongue
slipping along my flank.

I'm all
for it, of course, licking
the salty nipple
she offers, thinking this is the life
both of us lubricated
head
to foot, and her cunt, she says,
has never been so wet.
There's just one thing.
My cock
is taking a siesta, stretched
softly on my
lower belly like a lizard in the sun
and nothing she does
with her hands
or mouth
makes any difference.
The little limp bastard couldn't
scratch melted butter –
a disgrace to
all the stout examples of hardness
up and down the canyon,
even the talc.

Honey, she says.
I don't know, I say, and she rolls
up onto my chest,
one hand cupped over my cock,
gentle fingertips
strumming slowly under the balls.
She asks me if something's
worrying me, if
it's her – a litany
of delicate Socratic inquiries
which gets us no closer
to the truth but closer to each other.
It's probably those
morning quickies catching up with you,
she says,
we'll just have to get
you more ginseng, extra strength
this time,
or maybe some little blue pills,
a quick chuckle slipping through
her smile before
she lays her head on my chest.
The canyon grows quiet.
Air, heavy and thick as a comforter,
settles over everything.
I think we're going to melt, she says.
I feel it too –
everything loosening, the two of us
softening so fast
even a slight breeze could riffle
the story of its travels
into our skin.

It won't be long now, I think,
and neither of us
will fear getting scratched
no matter how hard
we might
rub against each other.

Sailing Along

The sand stretching as far as the eyes can see, and then going on
For miles, ravens riding columns of heat in the washed blue sky.

I shift us into four-wheel drive and the engine finds a higher note.
We haven't come to this place looking for answers – the wildflowers

Are gone, the sage is dry, the dodder has withered away, the creosote
Is long past its sweet air. We're taking a drive in the desert the way
   it's done

Out here, listening to the crackle of the all-terrain tires, the duet of
   straight six
And four-wheel-drive transmission as they sing our way toward the
   horizon

On our journey to nothing but the journey. We're travelling beyond
   everything,
To regions so remote that messages die in the air before reaching our
   devices.

At one point I ask my wife, how far, my love, before we should turn
   back?
Drive, she says, until the sand becomes water and we must learn to
   navigate

By the stars. Certainly a curious response considering the
   circumstances,
One I must ponder as the engine changes its tune and I shift to another
   gear.

The Beast in Decline Shares His Vision

Like to find
a place
with some land.
New Mexico,
maybe. Someplace
remote
with junipers
and a vista
for miles,
peaceful.

Be nice to
have a
woman, too.
One who doesn't
wear
makeup, who
hasn't read
a women's magazine
in years,
who
says fuck it
to
the internet
and
all the wretched
gizmos of life,
and won't
take any
shit.

Someone spry
and sharp
with
her tongue.

Someone who,
when I
get old and
start to
wobble about,
will stick
her head out
the
window
and yell,
hey,
old fart, the
outhouse is
the
other way!

About the Type

The typeface used in the text of this book is Meridien, which is a Roman typeface designed by Adrian Frutiger in 1957. Frutiger was born in Interlaken, Switzerland in 1928 and was apprenticed as a compositor at the age of sixteen to a printer in Interlaken and later studied at the school of applied arts in Zurich. While studying in Zurich, Frutiger concentrated on the art of calligraphy. His career has spanned the hot metal, phototypesetting and digital eras of typeface development. He lives in Bern, Switzerland.

About the Design

The cover and graphic design is by S.M. Burgess. Typeface for the cover title is 321 Impact, designed by Kenny Redman. Author's name on cover is a typeface called punksnotdead, designed by Eduardo Recife. The cover and inside photos were taken in Athens, Greece, June 12, 2006, at 10:43 pm, on Ermou St., by MLP.

 MICHAEL LEE PHILLIPS was born in Trona, California, and attended Fresno State College. Following that, he worked as a janitor, library clerk, newspaper reporter, feature editor, photographer and teacher. Except for extended periods residing in Ireland and Greece, he lives in California.

www.ingramcontent.com/pod-product-compliance
Lightning Source LLC
Chambersburg PA
CBHW051808040426
42446CB00007B/569